# ALPHABET
# BOOK

## A DK PUBLISHING BOOK

**Written by**

Lara Tankel Holtz

**Art Editor**

Melanie Whittington

**Production**  Kate Oliver

**US Editor**  Kristin Ward

First American Edition, 1997
6 8 10 9 7 5
Published in the United States by
DK Publishing, Inc.
95 Madison Avenue
New York, New York 10016
Visit us on the World Wide Web at
http://www.dk.com

ISBN 0-7894-2053-8

Color reproduction by Flying Colours.
Printed in Italy by L.E.G.O.

**About this book:**
When asked to count up letters in this book,
you should only count the ones in the pictures,
and not any that appear in the text or the corners
of the pages. There is also a complete word list at the
back of this book containing every alphabet object
to be found in the pictures.

# ALPHABET BOOK

Photography by Dave King

DK PUBLISHING, INC.

a | How many aces are under the album?  Find four angels. | A

Look for one artist and four airplanes.  Do you see the active athletes?

Find the aliens from a faraway asteroid.  Can you find two ambulances?

A | What is Alex's favorite animal?  Count five blue As. | a

**b** Search for a baby brushing his teeth. Spot a bear bib. **B**

Say "BOO" to the baby under the basket. Look for a ball and a blue boat.

How many babies are building with blocks? Find a baby blowing bubbles.

**B** Can you see a baby with a bare bottom? Find a bee. **b**

Count twenty Cs.

Can you find five carrots?

Find the cereal C on the cloth.

Spot a cat carrying a cake.

Spot a disappearing daisy.

Find the dinosaurs who want their dinner.  Do you see a doll in a dress?

What does the duck turn to open the door?

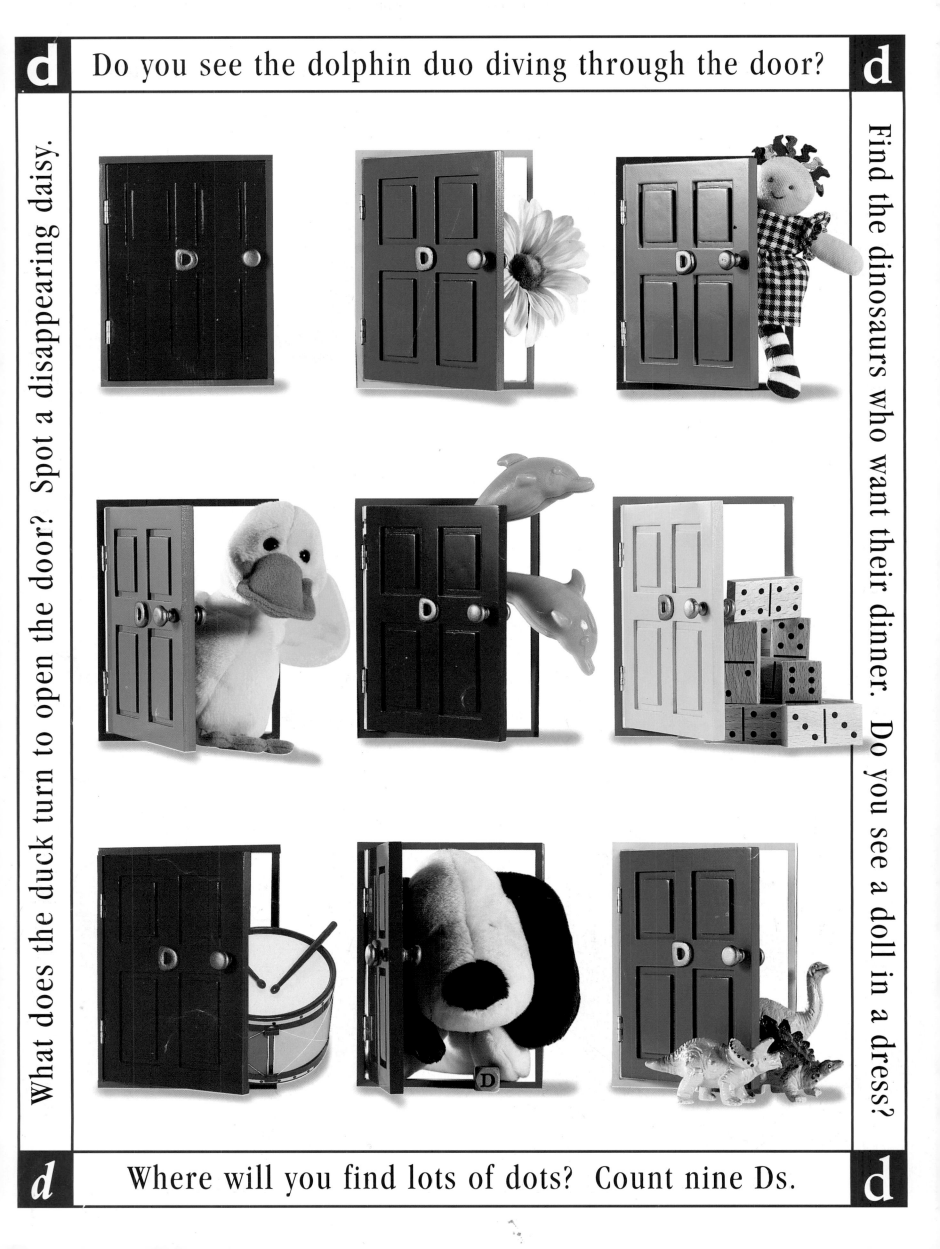

The flower is made of frayed fabric, fluffy fur, a fern frond, and what else?

A fly has flown onto the floorboards. Can you find it? Look for a frame.

There's a glossy grasshopper, a graceful goose, and a grumpy gorilla.

And there's a giant giraffe gazing over the gate at the gorgeous gazelle.

Help find two hovering, hanging helicopters.

Which object makes a horribly harsh noise? What is the house sitting on?

What is the huge heart hanging from? Can you find a hiding horse?

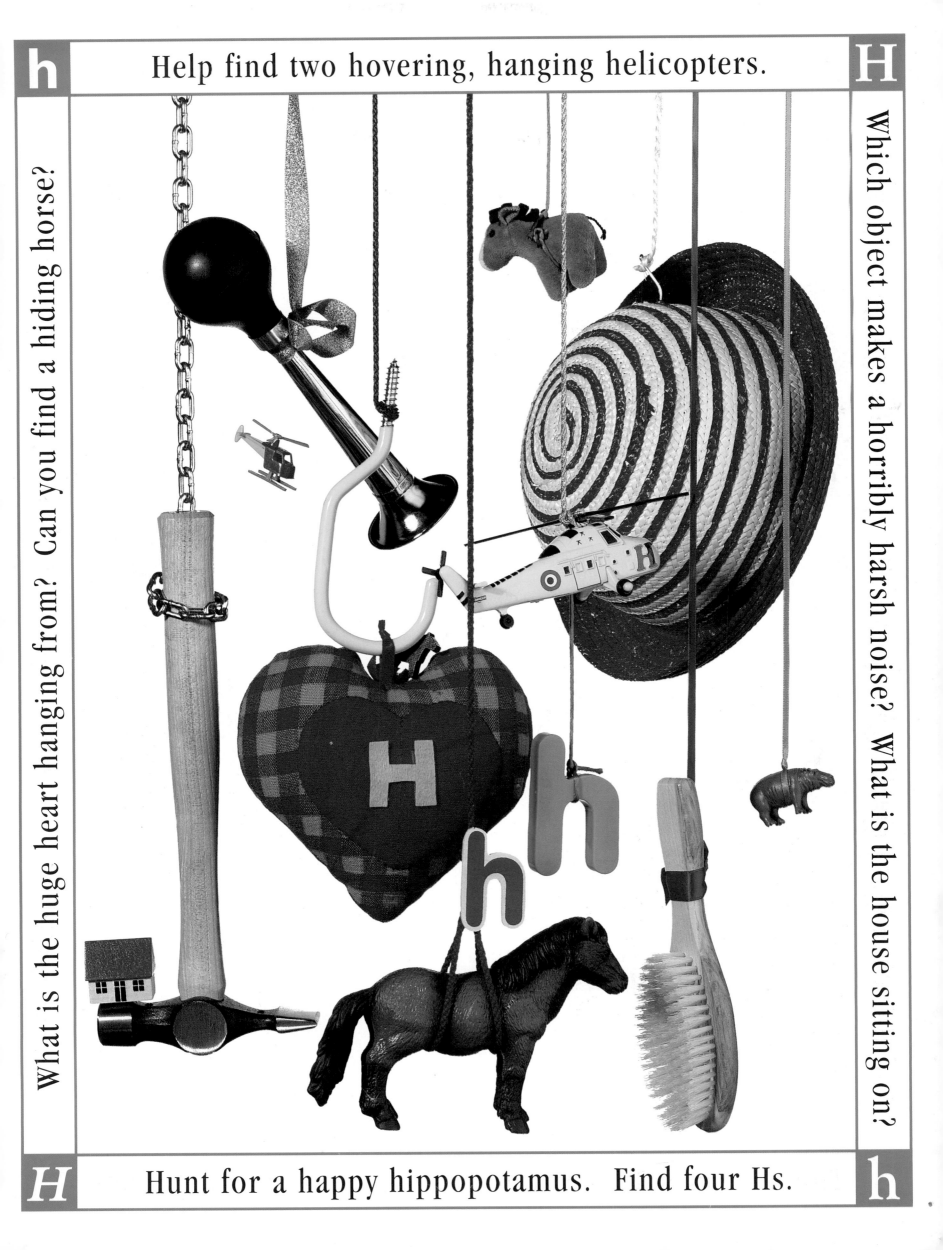

Hunt for a happy hippopotamus. Find four Hs.

Can you help identify the items imprisoned inside the ice tray?

Here's a jumble of jelly beans in a crazy jigsaw puzzle.

Try to find a red J, and look for a glass jar.

Count twenty jigsaw pieces altogether.

Now can you find a jaguar?

Can you find two heart-shaped jewels?

Once upon a time, a kindly king knitted a picture.

He put in two knives from the kitchen and a kangaroo he knew.

And when the picture was finished, the king went out to fly his kite.

He added a big green K and a pink key.

Locate a lost ladybug. Stop the lively leopard leaping up the ladder.

What is the lamb wearing around her neck? Look for a very large L.

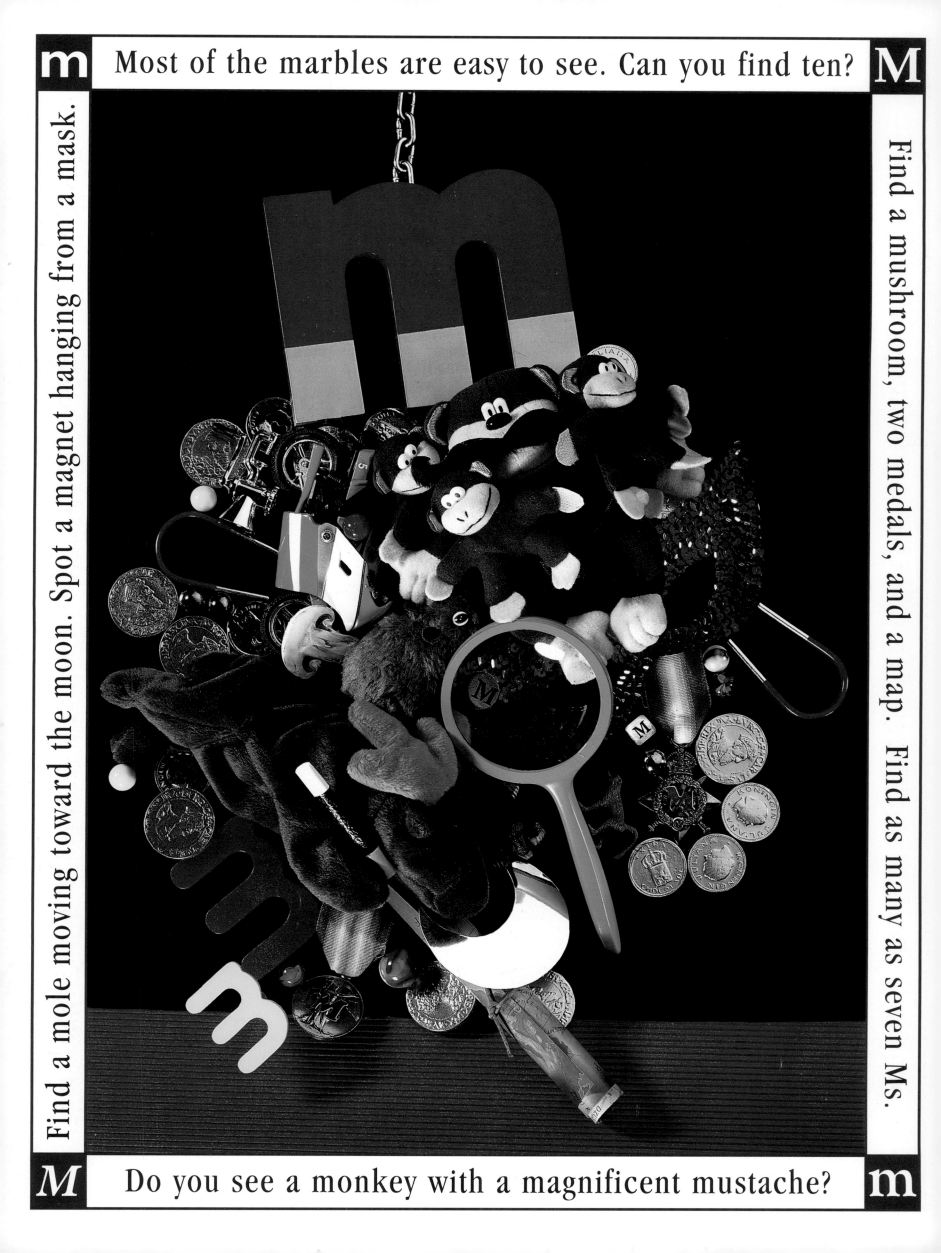

Find a mushroom, two medals, and a map. Find as many as seven Ms.

Find a mole moving toward the moon. Spot a magnet hanging from a mask.

Do you see a monkey with a magnificent mustache?

**Have you noticed the number of shiny new nuts?**

Now find five number nines. What was used to sew the needlework N?

Where is the nice necklace? Name the wavy N things next to the net.

**How many nails can you count? Find ten Ns.**

Overall, can you find five Os? How many oranges are above the octopus?

Count four whole oranges. How many legs does the octopus have?

Point to the person peeking. Find pencils in a pocket.

Look for two people wearing party hats. What is on the pirate's shoulder?

Where is the boy in pajamas? Spot a purse, two pink pigs, and two pandas.

Find a person eating a pizza. Spot two paintbrushes.

"I have a quest for you, my quite lovely quadruplets," said the queen quietly.

After a quarter hour the quadruplets were still quarreling. Can you help?

Find the ravenous rabbit eating a radish.

Can you count sixteen Rs?

Where is the rectangle of rice? Is there a rhinoceros in a row of Rs?

Can you see sixteen starfish scattered in the sand?

Spy a secret submarine. Find the stranded ship. Save the stranded ship.

Find the S.O.S. and save the stranded ship. Spy a secret submarine.

Spot a single seagull and two small sandals.

Find a scary skull and crossbones. Spot the snorkel.

Look for a teddy trying on a tiara. Find ten Ts in the toy box.

Find the teeth with toes and the tyrannosaurus taking a T.

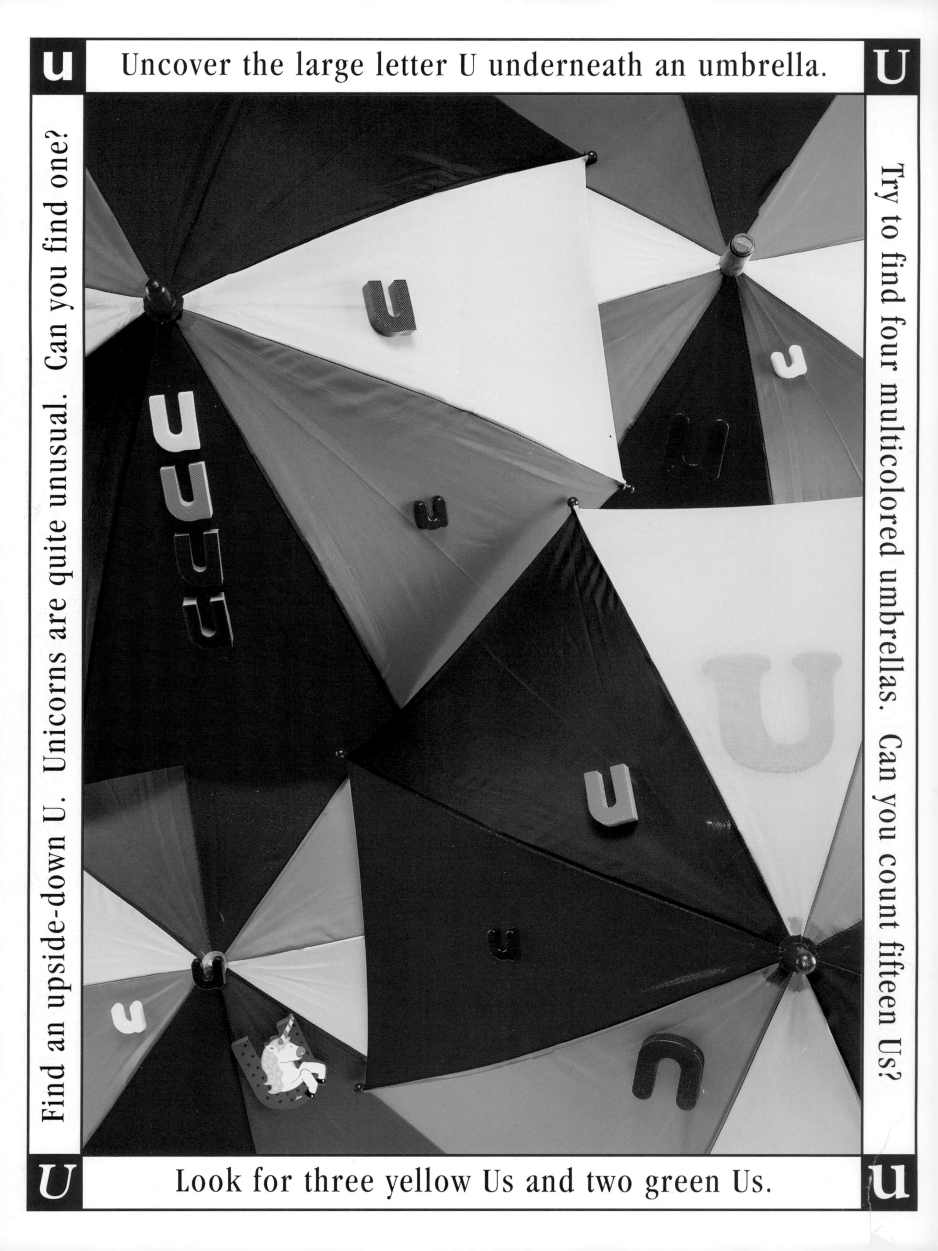

Uncover the large letter U underneath an umbrella.

Can you find one? Unicorns are quite unusual. Find an upside-down U.

Try to find four multicolored umbrellas. Can you count fifteen Us?

Look for three yellow Us and two green Us.

Visit the very vain vampire in his vault...if you dare.

What musical instrument does he play? Can you help find three Vs?

He has a variety of velvet cloaks and his best friend is a bird. What kind?

The vampire loves beautiful violets in a very big vase.

Where is the wandering wildebeest? Can you find a very wet wrench?

Look for two pieces of watermelon. What is swimming toward the wire?

This is an exceptional and extraordinary xylophone.

With this xylophone, you could play excellent tunes for a music exam.

There are an excessive number of Xs. Can you count twenty-three?

Have you ever examined an X-ray of a xylophone?

Do you think you can yawn and yo-yo at the same time?

Try yelling "YELLOW YO-YO, RED YO-YO, BLUE YO-YO, GREEN YO-YO."

Now, can you yawn, eat a yummy yogurt, and also yo-yo at the same time?

Can you count five yellow Ys and two red yo-yos?

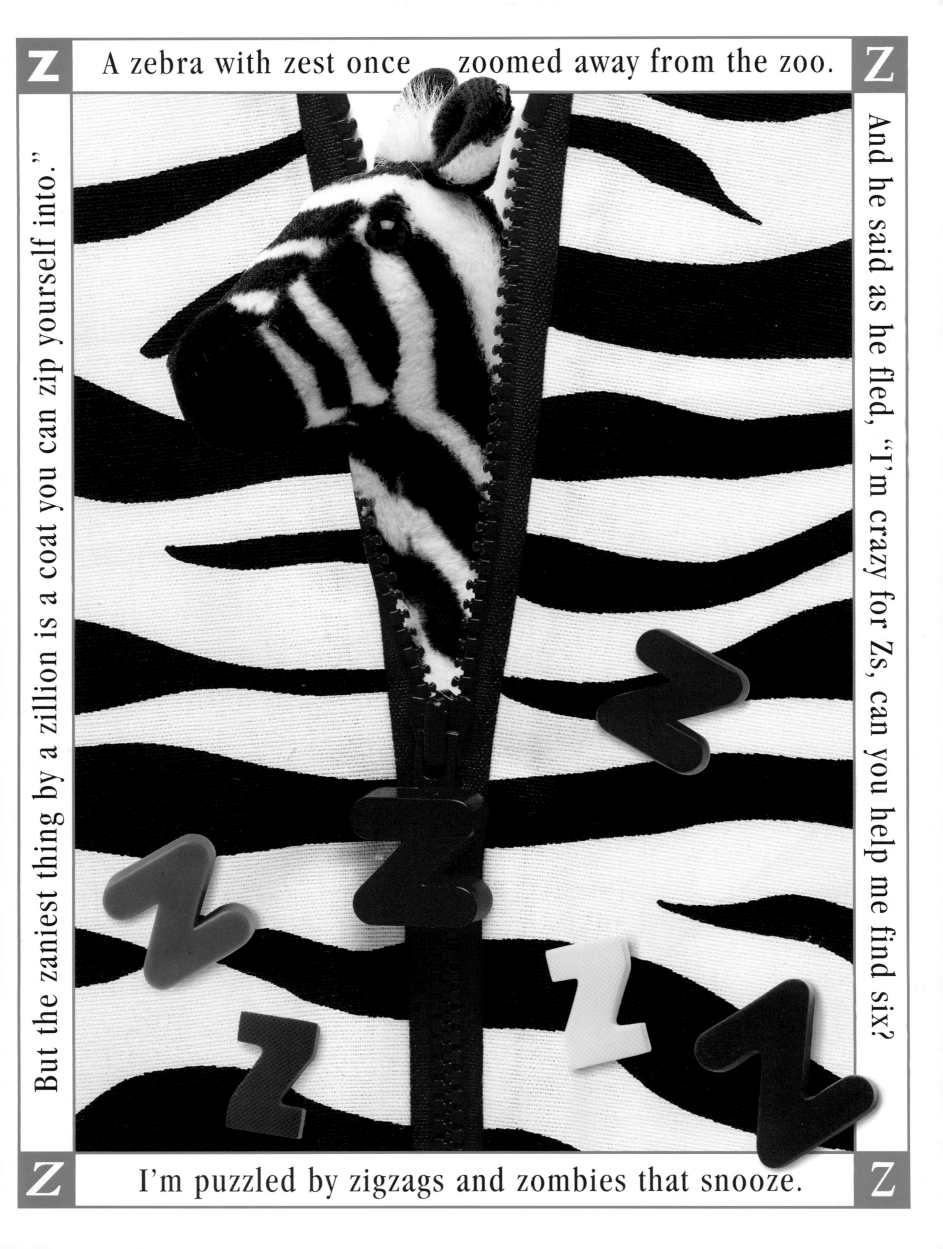

A zebra with zest once zoomed away from the zoo.

And he said as he fled, "I'm crazy for Zs, can you help me find six?

But the zaniest thing by a zillion is a coat you you can zip yourself into."

I'm puzzled by zigzags and zombies that snooze.

Z Z Z Z

# WORD LIST

Here is a list of all the alphabet objects that appear in this book. Can you read the words, then find the objects?

## A

aces
acorns
airmail envelope
airplanes
airship
alarm clock
album
aliens
alligators
ambulances
American flag
anchor
angels
animals
anteater
apples
arks
armadillos
arms
arrow
artist
astronauts
athletes
August
Australia
Australian flag
avocado

## B

babies
baby bathtub
backs
ball
balloon
banana
basket
beads
bee
bib
blanket
blue
boats
books
bootees
bottle
bottom
bubbles
buckets
building blocks
bunny rabbits

## C

cakes
candles
card
carrots
cat
cereal
cherries
chocolate
chocolate chips
cinnamon sticks
clocks
cloth
clowns
coconut
coins
colander
cookie cutters
cookies
cornflakes
cow
cream
crowns
crumbs
cube
cup
cupcakes
curls

## D

daisy
dinosaurs
dog
doll
dolphins
dominoes
doorknobs
doors
dots
dress
drum
drumsticks
duck

## E

Ear Egg
earrings
ears
Earth Egg
eggcups
eggs
Eight Egg
Electric Egg
Elephant Egg
Elevated Egg
Embarrassed Egg
Empty Eggcup
Enormous Egg
Entertainer Egg
Envelope Egg
Evil Egg
Examining Egg
Exercise Egg
Expensive Egg
Exploding Egg
Explorer Egg
Eye Egg
eyelashes
eyes

## F

fabric
face
fans
feathers
fern
fish
fives
floorboards
flowers
fly
footprint

fork
fours
frame
frog
fur

## G

garden
gate
gazelle
giraffes
goat
gold
goose
gorilla
grass
grasshopper
green glove

## H

hairbrush
hammer
hat
heart
helicopters
hippopotamus
hooks
hooves
horn
horses
house

## I

ice cream
ice cubes
ice skate
ice tray
insects

iron
island

## J

jaguar
jar
jelly
jelly beans
jewelry
jigsaw puzzle
jug
juice

## K

kangaroo
key
king
kite
knitting
knitting needles
knives

## L

lace
ladder
ladle
ladybugs
lamb
leather
leaves
legs
lemon
leopard
letter
lightbulb
lime
lion
lobster

lock
lollipops

## M

magic wand
magnets
magnifying glass
map
marbles
mask
meat grinder
medals
metal
mole
money
monkeys
moon
moose
motorcycle
mouse
mushrooms
mustache

## N

nails
necklace
needle
needlework
nest
net
nines
noodles
numbers
nuts
(hard-shelled fruit)
nuts
(to screw onto bolts)

## O

octopus
orange
oranges
orangutan
ostrich
owl

## P

paintbrushes
paints
pajamas
pandas
paper
parrot
party hats
patch
pencils
people
pigs
pigtails
pilot
pineapple
pink
pirate
pizza
plant pots
plants
plate
pockets
pointing
popcorn
present
puppets
purple
purse

## Q
quadruplets
queen
question mark
quilt

## R
rabbits
race cars
radish
railroad tracks
ram
raspberries
rat
recorder
red
reindeer
rhinoceroses
ribbons
rice
rings
robot
rock
rockets
rocking horse
roller skate
rolling pin
rope
roses
rows
rubies
ruler

## S
sailboats
sails
sand
sandals
sand castles
sea
seagull
sea horses
sea lion
sea urchins
seven
shadows
shark
shells
ships
skull and crossbones
snorkel
S.O.S.
spade
spots
stamp
starfish
submarine
sun
sunglasses
sunhat
sunscreen
surfboard
surfers

## T
tambourine
tape measure
teapot
teddies
teeth
telephone
tennis ball
threes
tiara
tiddlywinks
tiger
tires
toast
toaster
toes
toolbox
tools
toy box
tracks
tractor
trains
triangle
truck
trumpet
T-shirt
turtle
twenty
twos
tyrannosaurus

## U
umbrellas
unicorn

## V
vampire
vase
velvet
violets
violin
vulture

## W
watch
water
watering can
watermelons
whale
wheels
whisk
whistles
wildebeest
wire
witch
wrench

## X
xylophone

## Y
yellow
yo-yos

## Z
zebra
zipper

**Dorling Kindersley would like to thank:**
The pupils and staff at Summerswood School; James Edwards;

**The baby models**
Jack D'Cruz, Olivia DeSatge, Sahil Doshi, Charlie Holtz, Ali Miller, Thomas Skinner, Amané Sobue, and Lauren Stanton;

**Additional photography**
Gary Ombler (letters U, X, Y, Z);

**Model makers**
David and Sue Donkin, Hot House Models;

Ann Nicol for the clown cake; Rachel Tankel and Sarah Leader for the cookies and cupcakes; Jean Horne for the knitting; Milly Eavis for the felt objects; Sarah Charman for the needlework N; Stephanie Spyrakis for the Vampire face; Stephen Goknel for being the Vampire.